Original title:
Naptime Nibbles and Giggle Grains

Copyright © 2024 Creative Arts Management OÜ
All rights reserved.

Author: Vivienne Beaumont
ISBN HARDBACK: 978-9916-90-502-9
ISBN PAPERBACK: 978-9916-90-503-6

Drowsy Delightful Bites

In the quiet of the night,
Cookies crumble, a sweet delight.
Warm milk whispers soft and low,
Dreams take flight as flavors flow.

Cocoa swirls in hazy light,
Each tiny nibble feels just right.
Pillow clouds, we drift and sway,
Delicious charm guides our way.

Chill Vibes and Tasty Tributes

Under the sun, we share a feast,
Fruit and cheese, a vibrant beast.
Chilled drinks with bubbles rise,
Laughter echoes 'neath blue skies.

Savory spreads on wooden boards,
Friendship flows, and joy affords.
Moments pause as flavors blend,
Chill vibes linger, our time we spend.

Snacky Summons of Smiles

Popcorn pops in evening's glow,
Lemonade's sweet sip, ebb and flow.
Chips and dips set the mood right,
Every crunch brings pure delight.

Cookies stacked like towers high,
Each bite sends us to the sky.
With friends around, laughter grows,
Snacky summons, joy bestows.

Restful Revelry in Yumland

Beneath the stars, blankets spread,
Tasty wonders, our hearts are fed.
Cakes and pies in moonlight gleam,
Every bite fulfills a dream.

Sipping tea, we share our tales,
Warmth surrounds, as laughter sails.
In Yumland's peace, we find our place,
Restful revelry, a warm embrace.

Sweet Sips and Gentle Nibbles

Beneath the shade of laughing trees,
Sweet sips flow with gentle ease.
Crackers crunched on grassy ground,
Joyful echoes all around.

Butterflies dance, a soft parade,
As laughter weaves through sunlight's shade.
Cups filled high, and hearts so light,
In shared delight, the world feels right.

Mirthful Morsels at Dusk

As day turns gold and shadows play,
Morsels shared at end of day.
With every bite, a story spun,
Underneath the setting sun.

Candles flicker, soft and bright,
Anticipation fills the night.
With cherished friends, the flavors bloom,
In laughter's warmth, we banish gloom.

Laughter Between Soft Pillows

In cozy corners, laughter springs,
Between the pillows, joy takes wing.
Whispers shared in twilight's glow,
Each giggle leaves a lovely flow.

Soft blankets wrap our happy hearts,
As fondness sparkles, never parts.
Together we chase away the fears,
Creating memories through the years.

Chews of Joyful Rest

Evening settles, calm and sweet,
Chews of joy, a gentle treat.
With every taste, we take a breath,
In simple moments, love finds depth.

Stars emerge in velvet skies,
Resting heads, with sleepy sighs.
Bound by flavors, dreams take flight,
In serendipity's warm light.

Sweet Slumbers and Saucy Snacks

In the evening's gentle glow,
Cookies rest, all in a row.
Chocolate dreams melt on the tongue,
As sleepy lullabies are sung.

Soft pillows cradle weary heads,
Whispers of cake dance in their beds.
The warmth of fudge wraps round so tight,
In sweet slumbers, all feels right.

Marshmallow clouds, frosted and light,
Flicker like stars in the night.
While crumbs of joy gather around,
In this haven, peace is found.

Let morsels of joy forever stay,
As dreams of snacks carry us away.
In the land where flavors bask,
Together, we share our saucy snack.

Tiny Treats at Day's End

As twilight paints the sky a hue,
Tiny treats come into view.
Little bites of pure delight,
Promising joy by candlelight.

Cupcakes beckon with sweet charm,
Each frosting swirl, a tiny warm.
Cookies whisper, 'Have just one more,'
As laughter echoes from the floor.

Sipping milk, the stars take flight,
Underneath the soft moonlight.
Tiny treats in hand we share,
Creating moments, light as air.

With every nibble, we grow closer,
Sweet memories, our hearts expose.
In the hush of night, our lives blend,
As we savor these tiny treats at day's end.

Echoes of Playful Pastries

In the corner, a pie sits warm,
Crusty edges, a delightful charm.
Whispers of joy in every slice,
Wrapped in flavors, oh so nice.

Doughnuts spin with sugary glee,
Colors bright, as bright can be.
Eclairs filled with dreams so sweet,
Each playful bite, a lovely treat.

Cupcakes dance with sprinkles bright,
Echoes of laughter fill the night.
Each pastry tells a tale unique,
In our hearts, they softly speak.

From oven warmth to our delight,
Joyful moments take their flight.
In every crumb, a story played,
Echoes of pastries never fade.

Full Bellies and Fairy Tales

At the table, stories unfold,
With every bite, adventures told.
Pies and cakes, in laughter steeped,
In full bellies, sweet dreams are reaped.

Magical feasts of love and cheer,
As desserts melt away our fear.
A sprinkle of hope, a dash of fun,
Baking together, we all are one.

Every cookie holds a fable true,
With icing stars and skies of blue.
Sharing treats, our bonds we weave,
In fairy tales, we laugh and believe.

So gather round, let stories share,
In full bellies, dreams fill the air.
With every flavor, life's a song,
In our hearts, where we belong.

Blissful Bites in Wonderlands

In a garden where dreams entwine,
A sprinkle of joy in every line.
Colors dance in morning dew,
Sweet laughter fills the skies so blue.

Berries burst with a tender taste,
Every moment not to waste.
Underneath the sun's warm glow,
Magic lingers where we go.

Cheerful Crunches for Cozy Hearts

Rustling leaves beneath our feet,
Nature's symphony, oh so sweet.
Crunching apples, bright and red,
Whispers of joy in every spread.

Gathered near a crackling fire,
Friendship's bond, our hearts aspire.
Cozy blankets hold us tight,
Sharing tales into the night.

Afternoon Whimsy and Yummy Revels

Sandwiches stacked with love and cheer,
Every bite brings those we hold near.
Flavors twirl in a lively dance,
Each morsel offers a blissful chance.

Breezy laughter, skies so wide,
With every sip, we let joy glide.
Whimsy wraps our afternoon,
In the warmth of a bright balloon.

Savoring Soft Smiles of Slumber

Pillows soft like clouds above,
Dancing dreams we've come to love.
A gentle hush, the world at rest,
In sleepy corners, we're truly blessed.

Kisses of moonlight, a tender spree,
Whispered wishes set us free.
Counting stars, a joy so bright,
Savoring peace in the quiet night.

Dainty Morsels of Tranquility

Gentle whispers in the breeze,
Softly cradled among the trees.
Butterflies dance in the sweet sun,
Moments like these have just begun.

Petals unfold in soft embrace,
Nature's beauty, a quiet space.
Time slows down, the heart will sing,
Finding peace in everything.

Sweets Under Cloudy Blankets

Raindrops fall like gentle sighs,
Underneath the muted skies.
Warmth of cocoa, rich and deep,
In cozy corners, dreams to keep.

Fluffy blankets, tales retold,
Nestled in, we brave the cold.
Muffled laughter, sweet delight,
Chasing shadows through the night.

Frolicsome Flavors at Dusk

Golden hues as daylight fades,
Nature hums, the night cascades.
Crickets chirp, a soft refrain,
In twilight's glow, we feel the gain.

Savory scents from nearby feasts,
Celebrating with the beasts.
Joy in every taste we find,
Wandering hearts, forever kind.

Tiny Tastes of Serenade

Softly strummed beneath the stars,
Melodies twinkling like afar.
Sweetness drips from every note,
In harmony, our spirits float.

Cupcakes whisper dreams and hope,
Frosted wishes, gentle scope.
With every bite, the night unfolds,
Magic shared, a tale retold.

Mirth in Each Little Bite

In a world where joy resides,
Every taste a sweet surprise.
With each crunch, laughter ignites,
    Mirth in each little bite.

Fruits and spices dance around,
In every dish, delight is found.
Savor moments, pure and bright,
    Mirth in each little bite.

Chocolate drips, a silky stream,
Whipped cream flows, a dreamy dream.
Gather friends, it feels just right,
    Mirth in each little bite.

Life's banquet waits, a grand affair,
Sharing joy beyond compare.
Raise your forks, let spirits kite,
    Mirth in each little bite.

Hugging Flavors and Whimsical Smiles

In kitchens warm, where love is stirred,
A pinch of magic in every word.
A dance of herbs, a spice that beguiles,
Hugging flavors and whimsical smiles.

Savory stews in a comforting bowl,
Warm bread fresh from the oven's whole.
Each meal crafted, a tender style,
Hugging flavors and whimsical smiles.

Candied fruits and pastries so bright,
Colors that twinkle, pure delight.
Gather round, stay for a while,
Hugging flavors and whimsical smiles.

Laughter lingers, stories unfold,
In every bite, love is retold.
Together we share, every mile,
Hugging flavors and whimsical smiles.

A Symphony of Sprouts and Smiles

In gardens green, where laughter sways,
Tiny sprouts dance in sunny rays.
With whispers sweet, they greet the morn,
In joyful turf, new dreams are born.

Their colors bright, a canvas wide,
Each leaf a song, no need to hide.
With every gust, they softly sway,
Creating bliss in nature's play.

Sleepy Snacks and Glittering Giggles

Crispy treats in cozy nooks,
Cuddle close with storybooks.
Laughter bubbles, warm and light,
In these moments, hearts take flight.

Sugar sprinkled, stars align,
Each bit shared feels so divine.
Under blankets, dreams take wing,
In the nighttime, joy we bring.

Whispers of Sated Dreams

Softly now, the world is still,
In gentle breaths, our spirits fill.
Moonbeams cast their silver glow,
Where sleepy thoughts like rivers flow.

Wrapped in peace, the night unfolds,
With tales of warmth forever told.
In slumber's arms, we find our way,
To brighter joys of the new day.

Crumbs of Contented Slumber

When daylight fades, the night will hum,
With lullabies, we all succumb.
In cozy beds, our minds will drift,
Each restful sigh, a loving gift.

Crumbs of dreams, soft as a sigh,
Paint the darkening, starlit sky.
In sweet repose, our worries cease,
Finding solace, joy, and peace.

Tiny Nibbles

Little bites of joy, so bright,
Each one a moment, pure delight.
Tiny treasures, soft and sweet,
Whispers of flavor, a playful treat.

Crunching softly, they call my name,
Little morsels, never the same.
A dance of taste, a cheerful tease,
Tiny nibbles that aim to please.

Big Laughter

Echoes of joy fill the air,
Laughter bursts everywhere.
With every giggle, spirits rise,
A symphony of happy sighs.

In every chuckle, warmth ignites,
Shining brightly on chilly nights.
Together we share, moments so right,
Big laughter shines, a guiding light.

Ecstasy in Every Munch

Each bite a dream, a burst of bliss,
A savory hug, a flavorful kiss.
Textures dance, in joyful flight,
Ecstasy whispers, day and night.

The world fades, as I indulge,
In flavors rich, my senses bulge.
With every munch, a story told,
Ecstasy blooms, a joy to hold.

Smiles Sprinkled with Drizzle

A drizzle of sweetness, oh so fine,
It dances lightly, a sip of wine.
Smiles emerge, bright as the sun,
Together we savor, hearts become one.

Sprinkles of joy on a canvas bare,
Life's little moments, tender care.
With every taste, a rapture found,
Smiles sprinkle joy, all around.

Sweet Dreams and Crunchy Whispers

In the quiet of night, dreams take flight,
Crunchy whispers, soft and light.
Nibbles of hope, in slumber's embrace,
Sweet dreams linger, a gentle trace.

Each crunch holds stories, yet untold,
In every bite, the night unfolds.
Whispers of magic in the air,
Sweet dreams linger, everywhere.

Morsels of Mirth

In the laughter of friends, joy ignites,
A sprinkle of cheer, a dance of lights.
Moments cherished, day turns to night,
With hearts full of warmth, we take flight.

Whispers of secrets in twilight's embrace,
Laughter rings sweet, time leaves no trace.
Each morsel of mirth, like stars in the sky,
Together we flourish, together we fly.

The Sweetness of Snooze

In the arms of slumber, dreams take their flight,
Soft pillows cradle, a gentle delight.
The world fades away, as eyelids descend,
In the sweetness of snooze, all troubles suspend.

Clouds of soft whispers wrap 'round like a shroud,
Peaceful and calm, beneath night's soft cloud.
Time drifts away in this tranquil embrace,
In the sweetness of snooze, find your safe space.

Cradles of Comfort and Crunch

A cozy corner, snacks piled high,
With blankets wrapped tight, as the moments fly.
The crunch of good fortune, each bite a delight,
In cradles of comfort, our hearts feel light.

Familiar flavors, a warm gentle cheer,
Each nibble and bite, bring loved ones near.
In laughter and crunch, our worries are quelled,
In cradles of comfort, happiness swelled.

Joyful Bites at Dusk

As the sun dips low, in the evening's embrace,
Joyful bites shared, a smile on each face.
Fleeting moments captured, as shadows grow long,
With flavors igniting, our hearts sing a song.

Underneath twinkling stars, stories are spun,
Each morsel enjoyed, our souls weave as one.
In the hush of the dusk, we taste the delight,
With joyful bites taken, love feels so right.

Daydreams of Brownie Bliss

In a kitchen warm and bright,
Chocolate swirls in the light,
Fudgy treasures in a pan,
Whisked to life by a careful hand.

Sprinkles dancing on the top,
Melting sweetness, never stop,
Brownies baked to gooey dreams,
Endless joy in chocolate streams.

With each bite, a cocoa kiss,
Moments wrapped in purest bliss,
Daydreams linger, flavors blend,
In every slice, a friend to mend.

So let us savor, let us taste,
Sweetened memories, never haste,
In the heart where treats reside,
Brownie bliss, our joyful guide.

The Saucy Adventures of Soft Cookies

In the oven, magic brews,
Sugar dances, whispers, clues,
Softened butter, flour's touch,
Every bite, a love as such.

Chocolate chips like falling stars,
Melting dreams that travel far,
Golden edges, perfectly round,
In each cookie, joy is found.

Sprinkled laughter fills the air,
Scent of sweetness everywhere,
Adventures in the cookie jar,
Every taste, a shining star.

Share a cookie, share a smile,
Time slows down, live it awhile,
In each crunch, a tale unfolds,
Soft cookies, warmth that never folds.

Snippets of Sunshine and Scones

Morning beams, the world awakes,
Golden rays on fresh-baked cakes,
Scones rise high, a buttery dream,
Drizzled with honey, sunlight's beam.

Cranberries tucked in warm embrace,
Each bite brings a gentle grace,
Tea awaits on the table set,
With every morsel, no regret.

Sunshine spills on plates we share,
Laughter mingles with the air,
Scones delight with every crumb,
Joyful moments, hearts will strum.

In the garden, breezes play,
Days adorned in bright array,
Snippets of sunshine, sweet and warm,
Scones and smiles, our true calm.

Lullabies of Luscious Bites

Underneath the starlit sky,
Sweet treats beckon, softly sigh,
Lullabies of flavors sweet,
In dreams, we find our perfect seat.

Brown sugar whispers, chocolate dreams,
Filling hearts with gentle gleams,
Each luscious bite, a evening's gift,
As nighttime's bliss begins to drift.

Cinnamon dances in the air,
Comfort wraps us, love and care,
Every nibble, night unfolds,
Softly, sweetly, magic molds.

In the moonlight, we indulge,
Flavors blend with each sweet bulge,
Lullabies of bites, pure delight,
Rest easy now, and say goodnight.

Chortles in the Munching Moonlight

In shadows deep where laughter sings,
The moonlight bathes the joyful things.
Soft whispers of the night take flight,
Chortles rise in sweet delight.

Beneath the stars, the world a stage,
Where dreams awaken, hearts engage.
With every crunch, a tale unfolds,
In munching magic, life beholds.

The crickets play their symphony,
While laughter dances, wild and free.
In silver glow, the night embraces,
The playful joy, in hidden places.

So in the dark, let spirits soar,
With chortles, feasts, and so much more.
Moonlit munch, a sacred art,
In night's embrace, we share the heart.

Cravings of the Playful Heart

A playful heart beats in the day,
With cravings bright that lead the way.
In every nibble, joy unfolds,
A basket full of secrets told.

With candy dreams and chocolate streams,
The heart delights in sugar dreams.
Each playful taste, a burst of cheer,
A symphony that draws us near.

From frosted cakes to fruity swirls,
The magic spins in joyful whirls.
Craving smiles with every bite,
The playful heart ignites the night.

So gather round, let laughter ring,
With every nibble, feel the spring.
For cravings run, and hearts will race,
In joyful feasts, we find our place.

Hyacinths and Happy Nibbles

In gardens bright where hyacinths bloom,
The air is sweet, dispelling gloom.
Happy nibbles fill the air,
As bees hum soft, without a care.

Petals whisper in the breeze,
With tiny snacks beneath the trees.
In every bite, the joy of spring,
The taste of life, the songs we sing.

Cosmic whispers, nature's call,
As we indulge, we feel it all.
With every crunch, a tale entwined,
Hyacinths and happiness aligned.

As laughter dances, colors swirl,
In joyful moments, hearts unfurl.
Let happy nibbles take their part,
With hyacinths that fill the heart.

Flickers of Yum Under Faded Lights

Under the glow of faded lights,
A feast awakens, delight ignites.
Flickers of yum in every dish,
A savory dance, a tasty wish.

The laughter echoes, friends unite,
With every bite, the world feels right.
A tapestry of flavors blend,
As moments weave, sweet threads extend.

From sizzling plates to steaming bowls,
Each morsel feeds our hungry souls.
Flickers glow in ginger tones,
We gather close, forget our phones.

So let the night roll on and sway,
In glowing warmth, we'll laugh and play.
With flickers of yum to share and savor,
Under faded lights, we find our flavor.

Snuggled Delights and Delicious Chuckles

In blankets soft, we find our peace,
Laughter bubbles, never cease.
Warm mugs held in joyful hands,
Together here, our joy expands.

Whispers float in candle's light,
Tales of dreams that feel so bright.
Chocolate treats and smiles abound,
In this love, true bliss is found.

Dreams Whisked with Tasty Treats

Sugar sprinkles dance in air,
Whipped cream swirls beyond compare.
Each bite bursts with flavors sweet,
In every treat, new dreams we meet.

Soft cakes rise with hopes and cheer,
Laughter shared, we hold it dear.
Baking joy, we mix and blend,
With love and dreams, the flavors send.

Playful Pecks in the Stillness

Morning light through windows streams,
Chirps and flutters fill our dreams.
A gentle touch, a peck on cheek,
In quiet moments, love we seek.

Soft whispers ride the gentle breeze,
Heartfelt giggles put us at ease.
Nature hums a tender tune,
Together here, beneath the moon.

Cozy Croons and Savory Cravings

By the fire, the shadows play,
Timeless songs in hearts will stay.
Savory meals shared side by side,
In each bite, we take our pride.

Harmonies of laughter rise,
Comfort foods, and starlit skies.
In cozy corners, warmth we find,
Food for body, soul entwined.

Cozy Corners and Cheery Crunches

In cozy corners, shadows play,
Where warmth and laughter softly stay.
Crunchy snacks in hand we share,
Joyful moments fill the air.

Cheery crunches, sweet delight,
Bringing smiles both day and night.
Amidst the whispers, dreams take flight,
In our little nook, everything feels right.

Sleepy-Time Sweets

Stars are twinkling, soft and bright,
Whispers of dreams take gentle flight.
Sleepy-time sweets by candle's glow,
Cradled in warmth as night winds blow.

A sprinkle of sugar on tender dreams,
Melting away in moonlit beams.
Wrapped in comfort, hearts at ease,
Sleepy journeys drift with the breeze.

Whimsical Chews of Rest

In lands of wonder, where dreams dwell,
Whimsical chews weave stories to tell.
Soft and chewy, each bite a delight,
Carried on waves of sweet moonlight.

With every munch, a tale unfolds,
Of magic lands and treasures bold.
Restful moments fill the air,
In a world where dreams lay bare.

Snuggly Munchies for Daydreams

Snuggly munchies wrapped in cheer,
Bringing comfort, drawing near.
Crispy bites with flavors sweet,
In daydreams, everything feels complete.

As golden rays softly spin,
Munchies whisper, let the fun begin.
In laughter and joy, together we feast,
Creating memories that never cease.

Cheery Chomps of Afternoon Lull

In the sun's soft embrace, we lie,
Sipping lemonade, hearing birds fly.
Cookies crumbling with every bite,
Whispers of joy, the world feels right.

Laughter dances on the warm breeze,
As we munch on crackers and cheese.
Under the shade, we lay quite still,
Chasing the days, the heart can fill.

Delight in every crunchy sound,
Treasure in moments that know no bound,
With golden rays setting the tone,
In these sweet hours, we're not alone.

Dreamy Delicacies and Silly Giggles

Whimsical treats on a bright table,
Marshmallow clouds and a jelly fable.
Chocolate rivers with caramel streams,
Where every bite fulfills our dreams.

Giggling with friends over candy jars,
Toasting our joys beneath twinkling stars.
Sugar sprinkles paint our laughter light,
In this wonderland, everything's right.

Frosting mountains, sweet cream skies,
Every discovery a grand surprise.
Together we dance in flavors so bold,
Stories of sweetness waiting to be told.

Puffs of Playfulness and Sleepy Bliss

Cuddly blankets, cozy and soft,
Pillow fights, eyes drift aloft.
Giggles bubble in the evening air,
Dreams of adventures, without a care.

Moonbeams sneak into our room,
Casting shadows that gently bloom.
Sweets await in a midnight feast,
Where laughter lingers, and joy won't cease.

Happiness wrapped in chocolate delight,
A nibble of sweetness before goodnight.
Puffs of dreams on soft, fluffy beds,
Magic lives on in sleepy heads.

Embraces of Flavor in Twilight

As dusk settles in, flavors arise,
With spices dancing under the skies.
Savory scents, a warm embrace,
Gathering friends in a cozy space.

Gourmet bites ignite our delight,
Sipping warm teas, hearts take flight.
Laughter weaves through every course,
In this moment, joy is the source.

Cheese and fruit share the plate's glow,
Under the stars, stories flow.
In twilight's charm, we find our bliss,
In every flavor, a memory's kiss.

Whispers of Crumbs and Dreams

In the night, where shadows play,
Whispers dance, then fade away.
Crumbs of hope upon the ground,
In quiet hearts, they can be found.

Stars above, a twinkling seam,
We gather fragments of a dream.
Each one glows, a story told,
In the dark, a spark of gold.

A gentle breeze wraps round our souls,
Reminders of life's hidden goals.
With every sigh, a wish is cast,
Building bridges from the past.

In the silence, we take flight,
Chasing echoes through the night.
For in each crumb, a dream survives,
Whispers stir, and so we rise.

Slices of Serenity

Morning light spills on the floor,
Inviting peace through every door.
A cup of tea, a moment pure,
In simple joys, we find our cure.

The world slows down, the heartbeats hum,
With every breath, we feel the sun.
Nature's canvas, painted bright,
In every shade, we find delight.

Lost in books and quiet dreams,
Where every thought a soft sunbeam.
Slices of time, a gentle grace,
In their embrace, we find our place.

As evening falls, stars take their stand,
Serenity wraps us, hand in hand.
Each moment's gift, a treasure shared,
In slices of peace, we're always cared.

Laughter in the Afternoon Light

Children play in fields of gold,
Their laughter dances, bright and bold.
Sunshine wraps them in delight,
Joyous echoes fill the night.

Every giggle, a sweet refrain,
In this moment, we feel no pain.
The world a canvas, bright and wide,
Laughter flows like a gentle tide.

Clouds drift by, like dreams on the run,
In their shadows, we find our fun.
Underneath the endless sky,
Hearts are light, and spirits fly.

Afternoon whispers soft and clear,
In every laugh, we lose our fear.
Together we share this joyful song,
In laughter's arms, we all belong.

Tasting the Clouds

Above the world, where dreams take flight,
We savor whispers of pure delight.
Cotton candy skies swirl and play,
Painting our hearts in pastel sway.

Every breeze, a gentle hug,
Carrying secrets, wrapped in a shrug.
We reach for wishes, kissed by the dawn,
In the air, where magic is drawn.

With each breath, we taste the blues,
A canvas brushed with vibrant hues.
Floating higher, we embrace the sound,
In this realm, our souls are found.

So let us soar, let worries fade,
In the clouds, our dreams are made.
A sweet adventure waits up high,
Tasting life as we touch the sky.

The Cheery Snack Symphony

Crispy chips and nutty bites,
Salsa dancing in the lights.
Laughter mingles, flavors blend,
Happiness on every mend.

Chocolate drizzles, fruits so sweet,
Party snacks, a joyful treat.
Popcorn popping, voices cheer,
Every munch brings friends more near.

Chilled drinks in colors bright,
Raise your glass to pure delight.
Tasty tunes that fill the night,
Joyful echoes, hearts take flight.

Savory bites and veggie trays,
Celebrate in happy ways.
Every nibble, every share,
A symphony beyond compare.

Lullabies and Light Bites

Gentle whispers fill the air,
Sweet and savory, love laid bare.
Crackers, cheese, and fruits so fine,
Evenings wrapped in warmth divine.

Softly hum the evening tune,
Beneath the watchful silver moon.
Silky dips and nutty spreads,
Cradling dreams in cozy beds.

Tea so warm, a calming sip,
Every flavor, easy trip.
Softened lights, a gentle glow,
Whispers of love in ebb and flow.

With each bite, the day unwinds,
Comfort found in heart's designs.
Light bites dancing on the plate,
A lullaby to celebrate.

Doodles of Delightful Treats

Tiny cookies shaped like stars,
Colorful candies from afar.
Fruit kabobs with smiles so bright,
A canvas sweet, pure delight.

Marshmallow fluff and jelly beans,
Imagination bursts at the seams.
Pudding cups, a playful mess,
Doodles drawn in sweet excess.

Chocolate dips and sprinkles rain,
Joyful munching, never plain.
Artful bites, a feast of fun,
Creating smiles for everyone.

Taste the colors, share the cheer,
Every treat, a love sincere.
On this canvas, let's create,
A masterpiece that won't wait.

Cradle of Cozy Cravings

Cinnamon rolls and fragrant tea,
Wrapped in warmth, just you and me.
Soft blankets by the fireside,
In this cradle, hearts abide.

Buttered popcorn, movies gleam,
In this cozy, we just dream.
Peppered nuts and sweet delights,
Candlelit on winter nights.

Loving munches, laughter flows,
Every nibble, passion grows.
Cravings close, as whispers play,
In this haven, here we'll stay.

Sip the warmth, embrace the night,
Cradle dreams till morning light.
With each treat, a tale to weave,
In cozy corners, we believe.

Softly Chewing on Wonder

The sun dips low, shadows grow,
In whispers of the evening glow.
Softly chewing, thoughts take flight,
Wonders linger, sweet delight.

Gentle breezes caress the night,
Moonbeams dance in silver light.
Each moment savored, rich and rare,
In quiet corners, dreams laid bare.

Flavor of life, both bold and calm,
Time flows like a soothing balm.
In the stillness, we find our peace,
As hopes and fancies never cease.

With every bite, a story spun,
In the magic of what's begun.
Softly chewing, we embrace,
The wonder in each sacred space.

Munching in Moonlit Meadows

Underneath the silver beams,
We frolic light, immersed in dreams.
Munching grass and flowers bright,
In the heart of gentle night.

Stars above, a twinkling show,
Together, we let our spirits flow.
Each crunchy bite, a taste of bliss,
Moments shared in joyful kiss.

Whispers dance through softest air,
Echoing the joys we share.
In this meadow, wild and free,
Nature's song, our harmony.

The world asleep, but we awake,
Each delicious crunch we make.
Hand in hand, we roam and play,
In moonlit meadows, forever stay.

Pitter-Patter of Joyful Chomps

In the garden, life does sing,
Munching leaves, oh what a thing!
Pitter-patter, tiny feet,
Joyful chomps in rhythmic beat.

Beneath the trees, in shade so cool,
Every taste, a golden jewel.
In playful dance, we sway and glide,
With laughter echoing far and wide.

Crunching through the early morn,
With each nibble, new dreams born.
Scurrying critters, no time to spare,
In this banquet, we share and care.

Under sun and clouds above,
Every moment filled with love.
Pitter-patter, hearts collide,
In joyous chomps, we find our pride.

Blissful Cravings and Dreamy Smiles

A hint of sweet, a touch of spice,
Each morsel tastes like paradise.
Blissful cravings, deep and true,
In every bite, a world anew.

Dreamy smiles beneath the trees,
Savoring life's simple pleas.
Fluttering hearts, a shared delight,
In every moment, pure and bright.

Together we laugh, together we eat,
Life unfolds with every treat.
In this present, worries fade,
As blissful memories are made.

The taste of joy, the scent of grace,
In shared adventures, we find our place.
Cravings whispered in the night,
In lovely dreams, we take flight.

Dreams Served with Sprinkles

In a world where wishes gleam,
Children's laughter fills the dream.
Sprinkles fall like stardust bright,
Coloring the canvas of night.

Cupcakes dance on clouds so high,
Frosted rainbows in the sky.
Every bite a tale retold,
Sweet adventures, brave and bold.

With every sprinkle, joy ignites,
Chasing shadows, chasing lights.
Creamy rivers, chocolate streams,
Life is sweet as sprinkles' dreams.

So let us share this tasty treat,
With every friend we long to meet.
In dreams we bask, in sprinkles play,
Together, we will find our way.

Chasing Butterflies and Bready Delights

Through sunlit fields, we run and twirl,
Chasing butterflies as they swirl.
In the breeze, sweet aromas rise,
Bready delights beneath clear skies.

Loaves of joy upon the grass,
Golden crusts that softly pass.
We share slices, warmth, and cheer,
In every crumb, the world feels near.

Crisp edges, soft centers, pure bliss,
Butterfly kisses, a simple wish.
With laughter weaving through the day,
Bready delights lead the way.

As daylight fades, the colors blend,
In nature's arms, we find our end.
Chasing dreams on this sweet flight,
With butterflies and bready delight.

Chewy Laughs Under the Stars

Beneath the sky, the stars align,
Chewy laughs, a bond divine.
Moonlight dances on our faces,
In this moment, time embraces.

Candies shared, laughter rings,
In the night, our joy takes wings.
With every chewy, sweet delight,
We toast to dreams that feel just right.

Jokes beneath the twinkling haze,
Echoes of our childhood days.
In the dark, our spirits light,
Together, we shine so bright.

As dawn approaches, stars will fade,
But in our hearts, the joy won't trade.
Chewy laughs, forever ours,
In dreams we'll find the brightest stars.

Crunchy Whispers of Twilight

As twilight whispers through the trees,
Crunchy leaves dance in the breeze.
Underneath the fading light,
Nature sighs, a calming sight.

Soft shadows stretch across the ground,
In each rustle, magic found.
Crunching underfoot, a song,
In the twilight, where we belong.

Stars emerge, a glimmering guide,
With every crunch, our hearts open wide.
In this hush, we find our way,
Whispers of night, gently sway.

Through the dusk, we roam and wander,
In crunchy whispers, minds will ponder.
This twilight grace, a moment to hold,
In every crunch, a story told.

Crumbs of Joy and Wonder

In the corners of laughter, crumbs do fall,
Small treasures of moments, we cherish them all.
Whispers of joy dance on gentle winds,
In the heart of a child, this story begins.

A glimmer of sunlight paints shadows bright,
Sparkles of wonder in the soft, fading light.
Each crumb is a memory, sweet and profound,
Binding us together, where love can be found.

From cookies and cakes, to laughter so sweet,
In every bite taken, life feels complete.
The table is set, our hearts are aglow,
With crumbs of joy, let our spirits grow.

So gather around, let the stories ignite,
In the warmth of our hearts, we find pure delight.
These crumbs are reminders, of times when we play,
In the tapestry woven, forever they stay.

Harvesting Smiles at Sunset

As the sun dips low, colors burst in the sky,
Harvesting smiles, as day waves goodbye.
Golden hues dance, with laughter so bright,
Moments collected in the soft evening light.

With baskets of joy, we gather and share,
The warmth of the sunset, a moment so rare.
Each grin like a treasure, each laugh like a tune,
Harvesting memories beneath the pale moon.

The whispers of breezes weave stories anew,
In the garden of friendship, where love always grew.
As shadows grow long, and daylight's retreat,
We cherish these moments, when hearts feel complete.

So raise up a glass, as the stars start to play,
To the smiles we gather at the close of the day.
In the tapestry woven, our laughter will blend,
Harvesting joy, where the sunsets descend.

Tastes of Tomorrow

In kitchens aglow, the future is born,
Tastes of tomorrow, in each bite we're drawn.
Ingredients dance, flavors collide,
Let's savor the moments, let's take a ride.

With spices and dreams, our stories unfold,
A fusion of cultures, both daring and bold.
The simmer of hope in each bubbling pot,
Tastes of tomorrow, a journey we've sought.

From sweet to savory, the palette sings bright,
Each dish a promise, emerging from night.
We stir in our wishes, our passions ignite,
Creating a banquet, our futures in sight.

So gather around, with forks held up high,
For tastes of tomorrow, let's reach for the sky.
In every connection, each flavor we find,
The richness of life leaves no one behind.

Silly Soufflés and Playful Pies

In the oven they rise, a whimsical sight,
Silly soufflés, taking joyous flight.
With giggles of sugar, and splashes of cream,
Playful pies beckon, like a sweet summer dream.

The dance of the whisk and the clap of the bowl,
Each recipe whispers, to laughter we stroll.
Fruit filling a treasure, a pastry's embrace,
In the warmth of our kitchen, we find our place.

With dollops of whimsy, we swirl and we twirl,
Creating our magic, as flavors unfurl.
Chocolate or berry, we choose and we bake,
In our heart's little bakery, there's joy we partake.

Let's share in this laughter, in every delight,
Silly soufflés, and pies taking flight.
Together we savor, with warmth and with cheer,
In our culinary world, everyone's welcome here.

Playful Puffs of Whispered Snacks

In the breeze, the chips do dance,
Their crunch a tale, a little chance.
Puffs of popcorn, light and fair,
Whisper secrets, scents in air.

Dipping sauces, colors bright,
Each small bite a pure delight.
Laughter fills the twilight glow,
As snack-time tales begin to flow.

Cheese and crackers, side by side,
Sharing moments, joy can't hide.
Friends gather, stories shared,
In playful puffs, love is bared.

Charming bites, a fun brigade,
In every crunch, sweet dreams are made.
Under the stars, our laughter swells,
With whispered snacks, our heart compels.

Restful Bites Under the Stars

Under the sky, so vast and deep,
We gather round, our secrets keep.
Soft blankets spread across the ground,
With restful bites, pure joy is found.

Berries glisten, a sweet embrace,
In each bite, a soothing grace.
Chocolate treats, rich and smooth,
With every morsel, we find our groove.

Whispers float like fireflies bright,
As we savor each simple bite.
In the stillness, dreams take flight,
Under the stars, our hearts ignite.

Peaceful moments, time stands still,
Every flavor, every thrill.
Restful bites on a gentle night,
Together we bask in the starlight.

Tummy Tickles and Dreamy Delights

Tiny nibbles, laughter shared,
With every snack, love declared.
Gummy bears and cookies swirled,\nTummy tickles in a playful world.

Chocolate fountains, rivers flow,
Sweet delights that steal the show.
Each bite sparkles, joy ignites,
Satisfaction in little bites.

Fruity sips in colors bright,
Giddy grins in the fading light.
With each taste, our dreams take flight,
Tummy tickles through the night.

In these moments, hearts unite,
Dreamy delights, pure and bright.
Together we savor this sweet reign,
In the rhythm of joy, we feel no pain.

Joyful Snack Serenade

A melody of flavors sweet,
Each crunchy note a tasty treat.
Around the table, friends will gather,
In joyful snacks, our spirits can't shatter.

Chewy twists and salty fries,
Sparkling drinks that hypnotize.
With every bite, our laughter sings,
In this serenade, happiness clings.

Nutty crunches, a symphony,
Savoring bites in harmony.
Together we feast, our hearts ablaze,
In this joyful dance, we sing our praise.

With every snack, love intertwines,
Creating bonds like vintage wines.
Joyful serenade, under the sun,
In every flavor, we are all one.

Jolly Chitters in Cozy Nooks

In a warm nook, laughter gleams,
Chittering softly, like sweet dreams.
Cupcakes frosted, sprinkles bright,
Joyful moments feel just right.

Warm tea steaming, whispers shared,
With friends gathered, no one scared.
Stories weave through cracks in air,
Love and comfort everywhere.

The clock ticks slow, time stands still,
In these corners, hearts do fill.
A cozy atmosphere, we guard,
In jolly chitter, memories hard.

When laughter fades, we treasure more,
Those fleeting joys on memory's shore.
In cozy nooks where love ignites,
Jolly chitters, sweet delights.

Tickle My Taste Buds

Savory spices dance on tongues,
A taste of dreams that life now flungs.
Fruits and pastries, colors bright,
Every bite a pure delight.

Chocolate drizzles, creamy swirls,
A carousel of joyous whirls.
Each flavor sings, a happy tune,
Underneath the silver moon.

Crunchy, munchy, sweet and bold,
Stories of kitchens, long retold.
In every morsel, love unfolds,
Tickle my taste buds, pleasures hold.

From warm breads to frozen treats,
Life's sweetness found in each feast.
Explore the wonders on a plate,
Let flavors dance, do not wait.

Ever-Twinkling Treats of Joy

Glistening stars upon a tray,
Sweet surprises in bright array.
Sugary wonders, bliss in view,
Ever-twinkling, pure and true.

Cookies, candies, syrupy bliss,
Each crafted treat a gentle kiss.
Lifesavers, gummies, chocolate bars,
Their magic shines like little stars.

Baked with care, love's secret key,
Every nibble, hearts dance with glee.
Whirls of flavors, gifts of cheer,
Ever-twinkling, drawing near.

Through childlike eyes, delight unfurls,
In sugary realms, happiness whirls.
These little treasures, joy impart,
Treats of light that warm the heart.

Giggly Whispers and Small Delights

In quiet corners, giggles sway,
Whispers shared, brightening the day.
Tiny trinkets, joys concealed,
Small delights that love revealed.

A sprinkle here, a wink over there,
Moments caught in youthful flare.
Bright-eyed laughter fills the air,
Giggly whispers everywhere.

From little notes to lingering looks,
Magic lives in storybooks.
With every flutter, life feels light,
In exchanges sweet, hearts take flight.

Gathering treasures, small yet prized,
In precious moments, love is sized.
Giggly whispers and smiles unite,
In joyful realms, everything's bright.

Tummies and Tickle Trains

Tummies rumble, laughter fills the air,
Tickle trains ride without a care.
Whispers of joy echo in the sun,
Adventures await, let's have some fun.

Cookies crumble, ice cream cones sway,
Giggling together, we dance and play.
Every tickle a burst of delight,
Under the blue sky, everything's right.

With friends beside us, laughter is loud,
On this bright journey, we feel so proud.
A world of smiles, a glow in our hearts,
Tickle trains keep us from falling apart.

So come along, join the joyous refrain,
Let's ride the laughter on tickle trains.
Each giggle a spark, let worries be tame,
With tummies and tickles, we'll never be same.

Snacktime Serenade

Breezes whisper through the leafy trees,
Snacktime calls with a playful tease.
Fruits and nuts in a colorful spread,
Delightful nibbles, let's be well-fed.

Crackers and cheese, a crunchy delight,
Sunshine's warmth makes everything right.
Gathering round, we share and we laugh,
In this simple moment, we find our path.

Sipping on juice, sweet and so cool,
Laughter flows freely, we're nobody's fool.
With each little bite, our spirits soar high,
Under the vast and inviting sky.

As shadows grow long, we cherish this time,
Snacktime serenade, life's perfect rhyme.
Together we'll sing, with hearts open wide,
In the joy of the moment, we all abide.

The Cookie Cloud

Floating above in a sugary sky,
The cookie cloud drifts slowly by.
Chocolate chips like twinkling stars,
Filling our dreams, wherever we are.

A sprinkle of magic in every bite,
Warmth of cookies brings pure delight.
With every crumb, a sweet little song,
To the land of treats, we all belong.

In the oven, aromas dance and twirl,
Soft and gooey, they make our hearts whirl.
Gather around and share every taste,
In this cookie cloud, there's never a waste.

So let's take a ride on this fluffy delight,
With cookies and laughter, everything's bright.
Up in the sky where goodies abound,
Happiness grows in the cookie cloud.

Giggling in the Grainfields

Golden waves ripple under the sun,
Giggling echoes, we're having such fun.
In the grainfields, we run and we play,
Chasing the sunlight, the clouds fade away.

Tiny feet dance through the tall, green stalks,
Whispers of nature, the softest talks.
Butterflies flutter, in colors so bright,
Moments like these are pure delight.

We tuck ourselves in, beneath the blue sky,
Surrounded by laughter, we dream and fly.
With every giggle, the fields come alive,
In this hidden world, we truly thrive.

As dusk softly falls, we gather near,
Grainfields whisper secrets, we hold dear.
With joyful hearts and memories to keep,
Giggling in the fields, dreams take a leap.

Sleepy Snacks and Cozy Laughs

In a kitchen dim with light,
Cookies warm and oh so bright.
Chocolates melt in sweet delight,
As laughter dances through the night.

Pillow forts and stories shared,
Sweet surprises, none prepared.
With every crunch, a joy declared,
In sleepy moments, hearts are bared.

Milk and biscuits, perfect pair,
Dreamy eyes and cozy air.
Every nibble free from care,
In our laughter, love laid bare.

The clock ticks slow, the stars are near,
Snuggled close, we hold what's dear.
Through fluffy clouds of joy and cheer,
Our sleepy snacks, forever clear.

Fluttering Flavors from Drowsy Bakes

Butter whispers, softly stakes,
Dough that dances, gently quakes.
Cinnamon swirls in gentle wakes,
Fluttering flavors from drowsy bakes.

Sprinkles rain like stars above,
Each sweet bite, a hug of love.
Wrapped in warmth, like hand in glove,
With every pastry, hearts will shove.

Golden crusts and berry bursts,
Satisfy the sweet tooth's thirst.
In kitchen corners, joy thus spurs,
We chase the dreams our ardor spurs.

From pies to tarts, the tales unfold,
In every morsel, memories told.
With each soft bite, our hearts behold,
The magic in the warmth of gold.

Crumbs of Laughter Under the Covers

Under blankets, shadows play,
Crumbs of laughter lead the way.
With whispers shared till break of day,
In cozy nooks where dreams stay.

Popcorn kernels, salty sweet,
Tickled toes and giggles fleet.
Every snack, a chance to meet,
In our haven, laughter's treat.

Fluffy marshmallows, hot cocoa fun,
Tales of adventure, never done.
Grateful for this time, just one,
Chasing shadows from the sun.

As snores erupt, the night draws near,
In sleepy silence, hearts sincere.
With every crumb, we keep it clear,
Love's the laughter, held so dear.

Heartfelt Munchies of Mirth

In the heart of evening's glow,
Munchies ready, spirits flow.
With every bite, our love does grow,
Heartfelt joy in the undertow.

Nutty bites and fruity chews,
Memories stitched like fabric hues.
With every crunch, the laughter brews,
Together always, through all the blues.

Chocolate drizzles, rocky roads,
Sweet connections, soft love codes.
Hand in hand, we share the loads,
In heartfelt munchies, purest odes.

As the candles flicker bright,
We savor flavors, hearts in flight.
In every moment, pure delight,
Mirth is tasty, love's true light.